corn on the cob

tomato

onion

carrots

Insects & other Little Creatures

bumblebee

caterpillar

ladybug

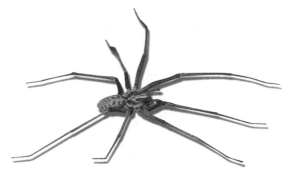

spider

butterfly

beetle

snail

centipede

In the Flowerbed

soil

daffodil

slug

pansies

bluebell

tulip

sunflower

Plants and Trees

pine cone

leaf

plant

tree

ivy

blackberry bush

shrubs

Pets & Other Animals

bird

squirrel

tortoise

guinea pig

cat

dog

rabbit

All Around the Garden

shed

grass

twigs

pond

greenhouse

flowerpot

table

patio

Working in the Garden

hose

watering can

fork

spade

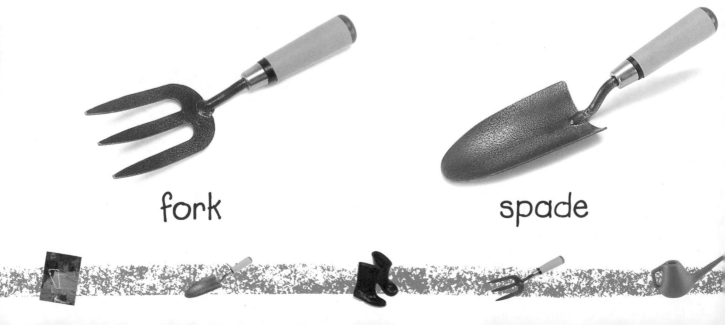

lawn mower

boots

rake

Picnic and Playtime

bicycle

plastic cups

kiddie pool

ball

barbecue

bucket and shovel

pineapple

In and Around the Pond

dragonfly

tadpole

water lily

goldfish

frog

reeds

newt

In the Grass

grasshopper

ants

weeds

clover

snake

dandelion

worm

buttercup

The Garden at Night

badger

bat

moth

mole